JUN 1 4

Smithsonian

LITTLE EXPLORER

SHARKS

by Megan Cooley Peterson

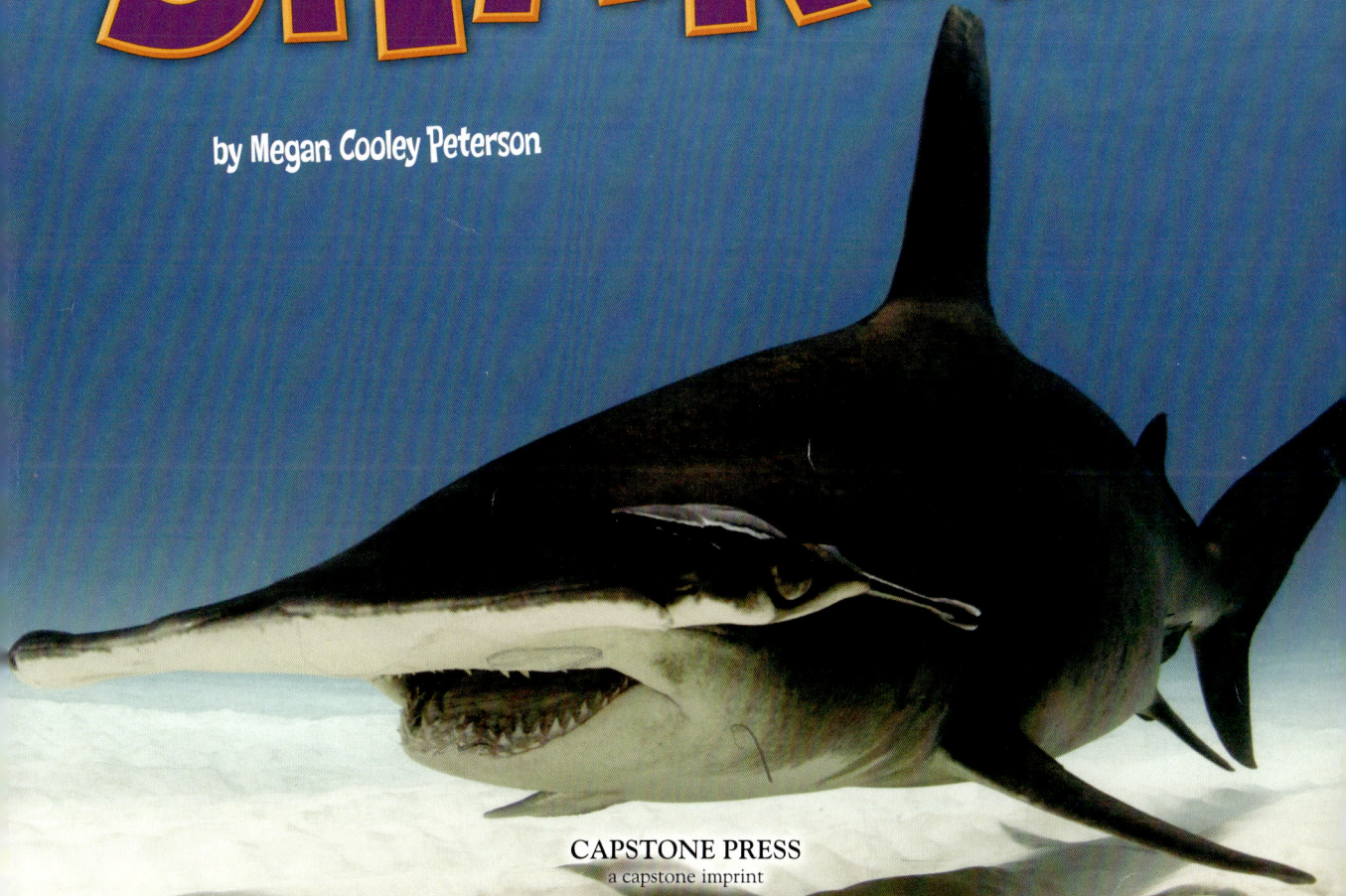

CAPSTONE PRESS
a capstone imprint

Little Explorer is published by Capstone Press,
1710 Roe Crest Drive, North Mankato, Minnesota 56003
www.capstonepub.com

The name of the Smithsonian Institution and the sunburst logo
are registered trademarks of the Smithsonian Institution.
For more information, please visit www.si.edu.

Library of Congress Cataloging-in-Publication Data
Peterson, Megan Cooley.
 Sharks / by Megan Cooley Peterson.
  p. cm. — (Smithsonian little explorer)
 Summary: "Introduces types of sharks and shark life to young
readers, including diet, habitat, life cycle, and myths"— Provided
by publisher.
 Includes index.
 ISBN 978-1-4765-0246-5 (hardcover)
 ISBN 978-1-4765-3540-1 (paper over board)
 ISBN 978-1-4765-3546-3 (paperback)
 ISBN 978-1-4765-3552-4 (ebook PDF)
 1. Sharks—Juvenile literature. I. Title.
 QL638.9.P438 2014
 597.3—dc23   2013000069

Editorial Credits
Kristen Mohn, editor; Sarah Bennett, designer; Marcie Spence,
media researcher; Kathy McColley, production specialist

Printed in the United States of America in Brainerd, Minnesota.
032013   007721BANGF13

Our very special thanks to Victor G. Springer, PhD, Senior
Scientist Emeritus, Division of Fishes, National Museum of
Natural History, Smithsonian Institution, for his curatorial review.
Capstone would also like to thank Kealy Wilson, Smithsonian
Institution Project Coordinator and Product Development
Manager, and the following at Smithsonian Enterprises: Ellen
Nanney, Licensing Manager; Brigid Ferraro, Director of Licensing;
Carol LeBlanc, Senior Vice President, Consumer & Education
Products.

Image Credits
Alamy: Carlos Villoch-MagicSea.com, 26, Chris Wildblood, 27
(top), David Fleetham, 14-15, Jeff Rotman, 9 (bottom), Mark
Conlin, 18, 29 (bottom), Photoshot Holdings Ltd., 23, Reinhard
Dirscherl, 28, WaterFrame, 11 (middle), 27 (bottom); Ardea: Pat
Morris, 13; Dreamstime: Jonmilnes, cover; Florida Museum of
Natural History, University of Florida, 6 (map), 7 (maps); Getty
Images: Auscape/UIG, 19 (top), David Yarrow Photography,
20, Photo Researchers, 17 (top), Visuals Unlimited/David
Fleetham, 17 (bottom); iStockphoto: cbpix, 11 (top), FtLaudGirl,
10; Science Source: Jan Hinsch, 22; SeaPics.com: Mary Snyderman,
21 (top right); Shutterstock: A Cotton Photo, 7 (middle), 16,
Alex Kalmbach, design element, Andrea Izzotti, 2-3, Annetje,
19 (bottom right), BMCL, 19 (bottom left), Brandelet, 5 (top),
dkvektor, design element, Ethan Daniels, 30-31, FAUP, 7 (bottom),
Greg Amptman's Undersea Discoveries, 5 (bottom), 21 (bottom),
Jim Agronick, 4, Krsysztof Odziomek, 7 (top), Mark Higgins, 8,
MP cz, 9 (top), nemlaza, design element, rachisan Alexandra,
design element, Rich Carey, 24-25, Shane Gross, 1, 32, shymko-
svitlana, design element, solarseven, 11 (bottom), Specta, 29 (top),
Stubblefield Photography, 12 (bottom), Teguh Tirtaputra, 21 (top
left); Visuals Unlimited: Dr. Wolf Fahrenbach, 12 (top)

TABLE OF CONTENTS

WHAT ARE SHARKS?...................4

WHERE SHARKS LIVE 6

TEETH AND JAWS 8

SPEEDY SWIMMERS...................10

SKIN AND SCALES 12

SHARK SENSES 14

SHARKS AND ELECTRICITY............16

FROM PUP TO ADULT 18

HUNTERS 20

FILTER FEEDERS....................22

SHARKS BIG AND SMALL............24

SHARKS ON THE MOVE 26

WHY WE NEED SHARKS.............28

GLOSSARY 30

CRITICAL THINKING
USING THE COMMON CORE...........31

READ MORE 31

INTERNET SITES....................31

INDEX 32

WHAT ARE SHARKS?

Sharks are fascinating fish.

They first appeared in Earth's oceans about 350 million years ago.

Most sharks are cold-blooded. Their body temperatures match the surrounding water.

Sharks are carnivores. They eat other animals. Some sharks also feed on dead animals.

Most sharks spend much of their time alone. Some sharks swim in groups called schools.

gills

Sharks take water into their mouths to breathe. It passes over their gills. The gills gather oxygen from the water.

WHERE SHARKS LIVE

Sharks live in every ocean on Earth.

More than 400 kinds of sharks swim along coasts and in deeper water.

■ = where great hammerhead sharks live

Most sharks live in warm water near the equator.

■ = where whale sharks live

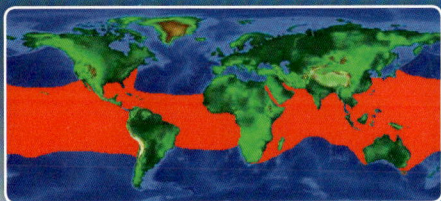

■ = where tiger sharks live

■ = where bull sharks live

Bull sharks sometimes swim into freshwater rivers to find food.

TEETH AND JAWS

CHOMP!

Sharks have sharp teeth and strong jaws. They use them to catch prey.

When sharks attack, their jaws pull away from the skull. A shark is able to open its mouth very wide to bite prey.

The sand tiger shark's long,
pointed teeth catch slippery fish.

Horn sharks crush the shells of
shellfish with their flat back teeth.

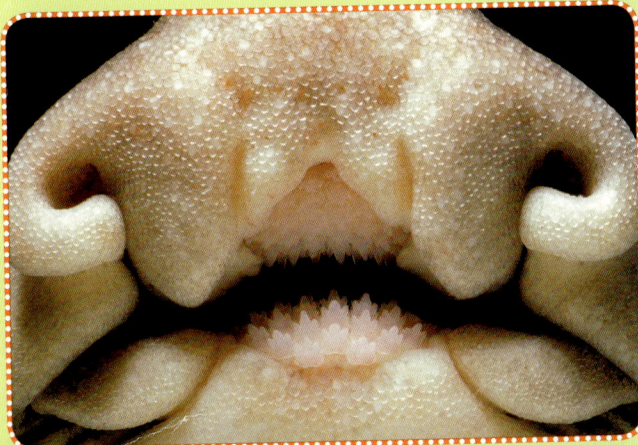

Picture

When a shark's
tooth wears out,
a new tooth moves
in to replace it.
Some sharks go
through as many
as 30,000 teeth in
their lifetimes!

9

SPEEDY SWIMMERS

SWOOSH! Sharks move their heads from side to side when they swim.

Sharks can't swim backward.

FINS

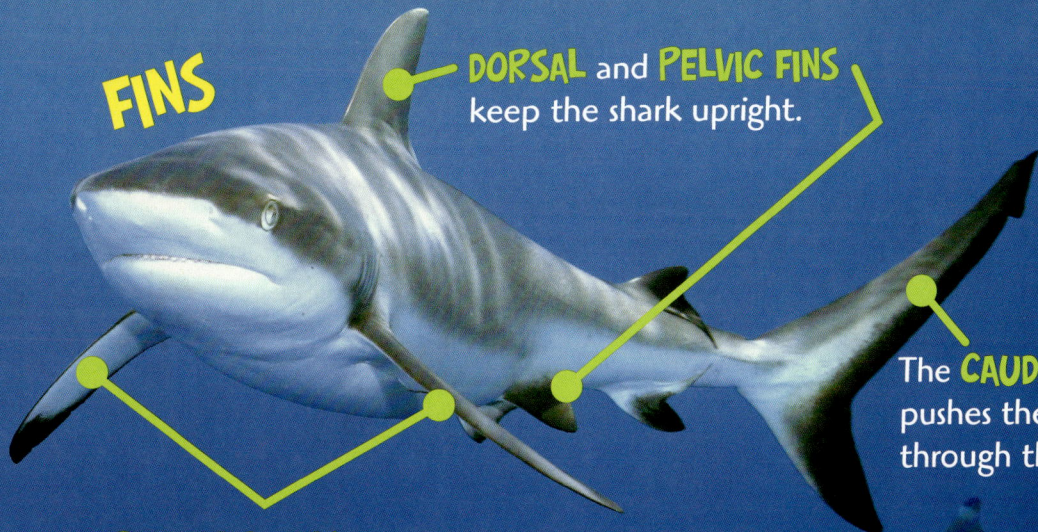

DORSAL and **PELVIC FINS** keep the shark upright.

The **CAUDAL FIN** pushes the shark through the water.

PECTORAL FINS lift the shark through the water as it swims.

A shark's skeleton is made of cartilage instead of bone. Flexible cartilage makes swimming easier. Your nose and ears are also made of cartilage.

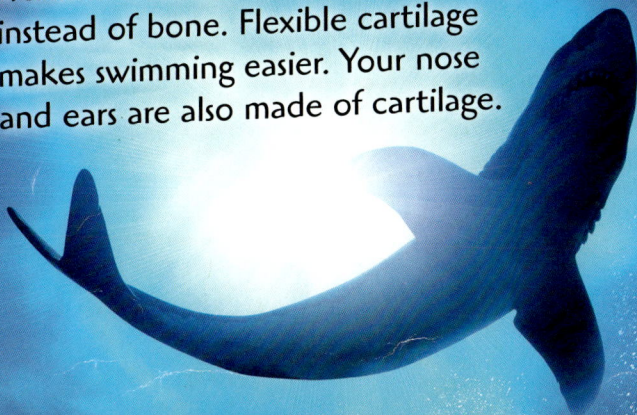

▲ The shortfin mako is the fastest shark. It darts through the water at 40 miles (64 kilometers) per hour or more.

11

SKIN AND SCALES

Tiny scales called denticles cover a shark's skin. Denticles look like small teeth. They make a shark's skin feel like sandpaper.

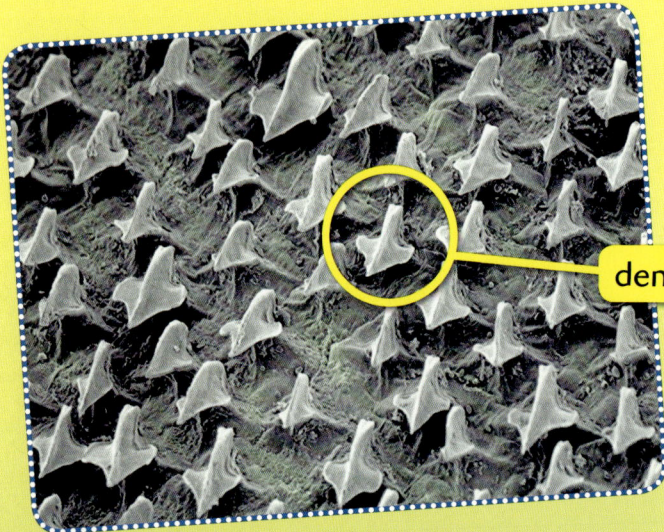

denticle

Most sharks have darker skin on top and lighter skin on bottom. When viewed from above, their dark skin blends in with the ocean floor. This coloring helps most sharks sneak up on prey.

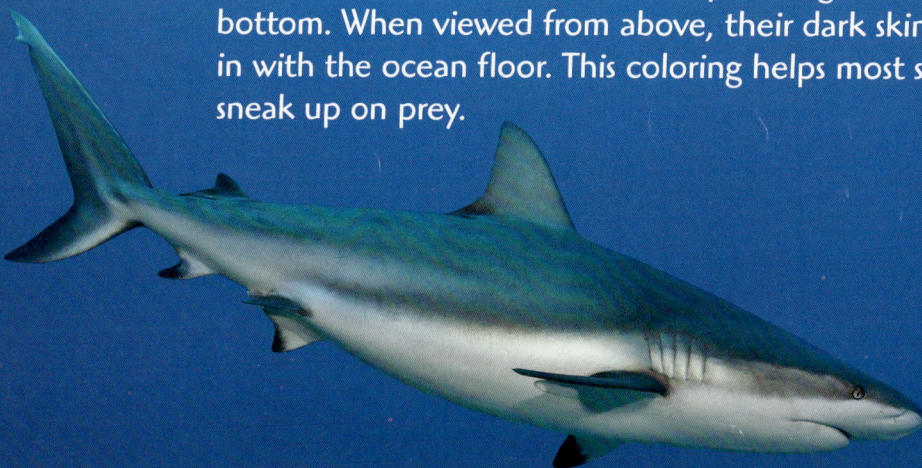

Denticles come in many shapes and sizes.
They act like armor to protect sharks.

Water flows smoothly over denticles,
which helps sharks swim fast.

SHARK SENSES

A shark's senses help it find
food and stay safe.

TOUCH
A special organ runs under a
shark's skin from its tail to
its head. This organ can
feel movements made
by swimming prey.

HEARING
Tiny holes on the top of a shark's head lead to its ears. Most sharks can hear sounds many miles away.

SIGHT
A shark's eyes sit on either side of its head. Sharks can see in almost every direction at once.

SMELL
Great white sharks can smell small amounts of blood up to 3 miles (5 km) away.

TASTE
Sharks bite prey to find out if it tastes like something they want to eat.

SHARKS AND ELECTRICITY

All living things give off small amounts of electricity.

pores

Sharks have tiny pores in their snouts that can feel electricity.

They use these pores to find prey hidden in the sand.

Sharks can feel electricity from prey up to 1 foot (30 centimeters) away.

Hammerhead sharks move their heads over the seabed to find buried stingrays.

FROM PUP TO ADULT

Almost half of all types of sharks lay eggs.
The rest give birth to live young.

egg

shark pup

All shark pups live and
grow on their own.

PUPS IN A LITTER	
bull sharks	7 to 12 pups
lemon sharks	6 to 18 pups
piked dogfish	2 to 16 pups

Zebra shark pups are born with striped skin. The stripes help them hide in seaweed as they grow.

Many female sharks lay eggs in tough cases. These cases keep the young safe before they hatch.

Some shark egg cases have cords on the ends. These cords attach the egg cases to rocks or seaweed to keep them hidden.

Sharks live about 25 years. Some types may live much longer.

HUNTERS

Sharks are born to hunt. Some sharks chase prey. Others blend in with their surroundings and wait for food to come to them.

Most sharks can't chew. They swallow their food whole or in chunks.

Great white sharks leap up to attack seals swimming on the surface.

Tiny bits of skin that look like seaweed hang from wobbegong sharks' snouts. Sometimes prey nibble on the sharks' skin. Then the sharks gobble them up.

Longnose sharks have sharp barbels on their snouts. They run the barbels along the seabed to find small fish hidden in the sand.

Tiger sharks are nicknamed "the trash cans of the sea." They will try to eat almost anything. Scientists have found clothing, license plates, and paint cans in their stomachs.

FILTER FEEDERS

Not all sharks hunt for food.

Basking sharks, whale sharks, and megamouth sharks are filter feeders. They mostly eat tiny sea plants and animals called plankton.

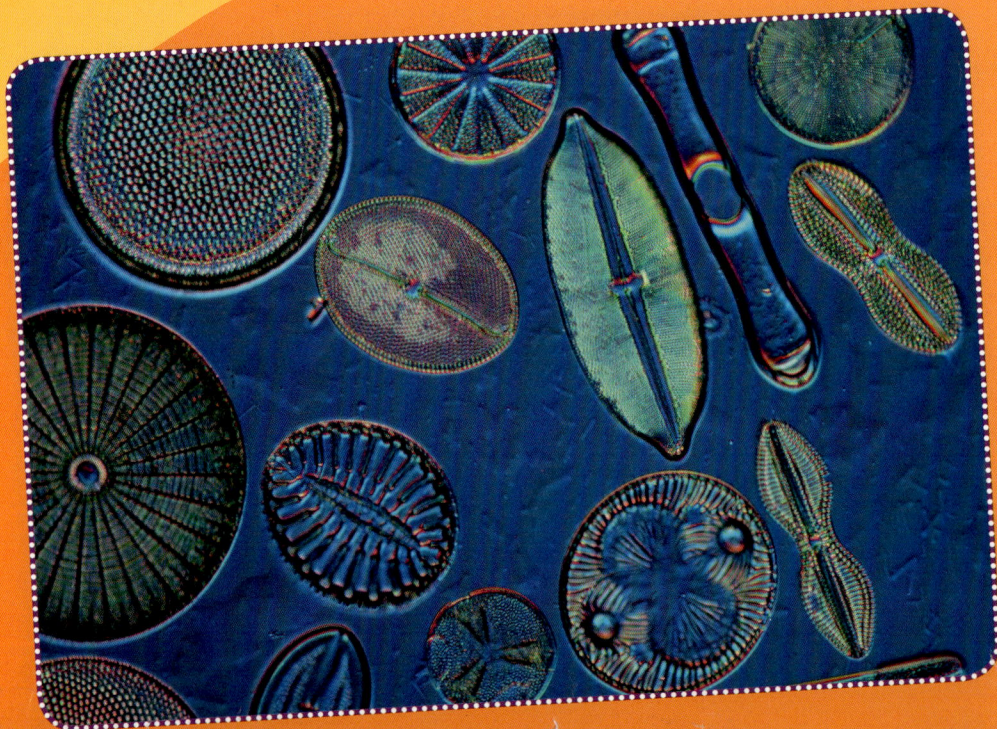

Some plankton are too tiny to see with the naked eye. They look very colorful under a microscope.

Filter feeders swim with their huge mouths open to catch the plankton.

Water flows through **GILL RAKERS** inside the shark's mouth. The gill rakers strain plankton from the water for the shark to eat.

SHARKS BIG AND SMALL

Whale sharks can grow as big as school buses.

whale shark: 40–65 feet (12–20 meters)

The whale shark is the world's largest fish.

bull shark: 11.5 feet (3.5 m)

great white shark: 24 feet (7.3 m)

diver:
6 feet (1.8 m)

nurse shark:
8.25 feet (2.75 m)

tiger shark: 25 feet (7.6 m)

great hammerhead shark:
19.5 feet (6 m)

Some sharks are
so small you can hold
them in your hands!

The dwarf lantern shark is one
of the world's smallest sharks.

6–7 inches (16–19 cm)

mako shark: 11.4 feet (3.8 m)

SHARKS ON THE MOVE

How do sharks find their way around the world's oceans?

Scientists believe they follow Earth's magnetic field.

Many sharks migrate to mate, give birth, and find food.

In 2003 a great white traveled more than 12,000 miles (19,300 km) in 99 days. Scientists still aren't sure exactly why great whites migrate.

Female great hammerheads move into cooler water in the summer to give birth.

Not all sharks migrate. The nurse shark never swims far from its home area.

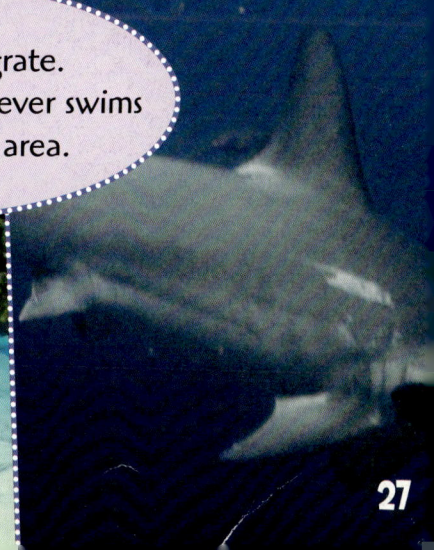

WHY WE NEED SHARKS

Some people fear sharks. But they are helpful ocean creatures. They clean the ocean by eating old, sick, and dead animals.

Sharks don't often attack humans. In fact, you are more likely to be bitten by another human than a shark!

Sharks are an important part of the ocean's ecosystem.

tracking tag

Scientists still have much to learn about sharks. They attach tracking tags to sharks in order to learn more about these amazing creatures.

GLOSSARY

armor—bones, scales, and skin that some animals have on their bodies for protection

carnivore—an animal that eats only meat

cartilage—the strong, bendable material that forms some parts of the skeleton on humans and animals

coast—land next to an ocean or sea

ecosystem—a group of animals and plants that work together with their surroundings

electricity—a natural force that can be used to make light and heat or to make machines work

equator—an imaginary line around the middle of Earth; it divides the northern and southern hemispheres

freshwater—water that does not have salt

magnetic field—an area of moving electrical currents that affects other objects

mate—when a male and female join together to produce young

migrate—to travel a long distance from one place to another on a regular basis

oxygen—a colorless gas that people and animals breathe; humans and animals need oxygen to live

pore—one of the tiny holes in your skin through which you sweat; sharks have pores in their noses that can feel electricity

prey—an animal hunted by another animal for food

pup—a young shark

CRITICAL THINKING USING THE COMMON CORE

The author writes about shark denticles on pages 12 and 13. How do denticles help sharks? Give at least three details from the text. (Key Ideas and Details)

Why is the tiger shark called "the trash can of the sea"? (Craft and Structure)

Look at the maps on pages 6 and 7. Explain what you can learn about sharks from studying the maps. (Integration of Knowledge and Ideas)

READ MORE

Arnosky, Jim. *All about Sharks.* New York: Scholastic, 2008.

Markle, Sandra. *Sharks: Biggest! Littlest!* Honesdale, Pa.: Boyds Mill Press, 2011.

Nuzzolo, Deborah. *Great White Shark.* Sharks. Mankato, Minn.: Capstone Press, 2009.

INTERNET SITES

FactHound offers a safe, fun way to find Internet sites related to this book. All of the sites on FactHound have been researched by our staff.

Here's all you do:

Visit *www.facthound.com*

Type in this code: 9781476502465

INDEX

barbels, 21
basking sharks, 22
birth, 18–19, 27
bull sharks, 7, 18, 24

carnivores, 4
cartilage, 11
cold-blooded, 4

denticles, 12–13
dwarf lantern sharks, 25

ears, 15
eggs, 18–19
electricity, 16–17
equator, 6
eyes, 15

filter feeders, 22–23
fins, 11
food, 4, 14–15, 20, 22, 26
freshwater, 7

gill rakers, 23
gills, 5
great hammerhead sharks,
   6, 17, 25, 27
great white sharks, 15, 20,
   24, 26

horn sharks, 9

jaws, 8

lemon sharks, 18
life span, 19
longnose sharks, 21

mako sharks, 11, 25
mating, 26
megamouth sharks, 22
migration, 26–27
mouths, 5, 8, 23

nurse sharks, 25, 27

oxygen, 5

piked dogfish sharks, 18
plankton, 22–23
pores, 16
prey, 8–9, 12, 14–15,
   16–17, 20, 21
protection, 13
pups, 18–19

ranges, 6–7

sand tiger sharks, 9
scales, 12
schools, 5
senses, 14–15
shortfin mako sharks, 11
sizes, 24–25
skeletons, 11
skin, 12, 14, 19, 21
snouts, 16, 21
speed, 11, 12
swimming, 10–11, 13

tail, 14
teeth, 8–9
tiger sharks, 7, 21, 25
tracking tags, 29

whale sharks, 7, 22, 24
wobbegong sharks, 21

zebra sharks, 19